Electric Rats in a Neon Gutter
Poems, Songs and Stories

by Luis Galindo

Mr. Galindo is a friend of *eljamberoo.com* and *flapperhouse.com*.

Photo of Mr. Galindo by Todd Pate.

To my Belia Rios Galindo and Luis F. Galindo Jr., for all their love and support.

Table of Contents

Round and Round

The conversation started the night before.

Awkward pauses and staring at each other for what seemed like way too long over dinner.

Trying desperately to glean some knowledge of how he was doing with her.

Trying to interpret every inflection of speech, every gesture, every breath.

The evening progressed into a long walk down her quiet street.

Up two flights of stairs. Unlocking the door. Her cats coming close to greet them. Into her living room for the obligatory couch talk until one of them took the next step. The step was mutual. They inched closer, their noses almost touching. The brief recognition before the kiss. The closing of her eyes before their lips met, before their teeth clicked, before their tongues swam together in their skulls.

The first kiss.

Deep exhalations of passion running like horses from their corral, the quick and hungry unbuttoning of clothes, the smell of dinner on the breath, the up close

Electric Rats in a Neon Gutter

and personal dance with each other's scent, senses, bodies and time.

The backward walk to the bedroom while connected at the mouth.

The deep dip in the center of the mattress.

The explosion.

The exhaustion.

Quiet in the sheets and staring at the ceiling as cats scurried and distant voices on the street below lulled him to a deep and hopeful sleep.

This new lover clinging to his body.

The conversation was completed the following morning over breakfast.

She sat him down at her two chair table in the kitchen. She made him coffee with a French press.

She stroked his hair and kissed his forehead after she poured.

They looked at each other for some time.

He couldn't tell what she was thinking. Finally she opened her mouth and said, "Don't worry darlin', I like you way too much to do anything as cruel as fall in love with you."

The coffee was steaming.

She shrugged her shoulders and smiled a half smile.

She appeared different somehow sitting there in the thousand watt sunlight.

He looked at his plate. A half eaten bagel and a few crushed berries remained in a blue and red puddle.

A leaf blower hummed outside.

For some reason he thought of his youth and of church. Of the unpaid bills sitting on his desk. He thought of how much gas was in his truck and of the traffic on Sunset boulevard. Anything to avoid the truth of the morning.

The sun shot through the window as certain as the results of an election.

This town was not his home and he never felt it more clearly in all of his time there than this very moment.

She sat across from him in silence, checking her phone. She got up from the table and walked to her bedroom.

Electric Rats in a Neon Gutter

He sipped his coffee.

He leaned back in the chair and sighed and the world kept spinning on its goddamned axis.

The Words of the Velveteen Angel

The velveteen angel
drugged my courage
and sent my confusion
into the hall
to cower
by the stairwell
and sob
like a defrocked priest.
Other worldly red light murmurs
in ancient shadows
tore my resolve to ribbons.
My fortitude was ossified.
My suspicion leapt
from the highest ledge
it could find
in the motel of my lust.
It broke itself on midnight streets
gleaming with the tears
of the lonely
hard as my denial
and as unexpected as the truth
in the mouth
of a senator.
"You won't kiss me"
she said
"You don't have the courage.
I have stolen your bravery and there is
very little you can do about it now."
I fell into her trap

Electric Rats in a Neon Gutter

I jumped her electric fence
and committed
grand theft of the moment
kissing her hard
nothing more perfect
nothing was but that.
We extinguished eternity's fuse
and danced
with the Gods
at last.

The Impossibility of Love, the Moments, the Night and You

I write this poem in ashes, rosewater and blue bird's blood.

Upon the altar I built to your apotheosis.

Upon a green promise made in novice nocturnes.

I swore to you over cocaine and red wine
that I knew you were my soul mate.

I swore to you over sober huevos rancheros
on a silver Sunday morning that my love was eternal.

I sang you songs in the Spanish Harlem night while
eight million fuses burned in electric longing.

I rigged the clocks to chime "Love Me Tender" every
time you walked through the door.

I whispered, "I love you" in your slightly deaf ear as
hard as gasoline, behind your raven waterfall locks.

I shouted your name in the lonely Gotham Winter my
voice was crystal, vapor, and doom on 108th and Lex.

That summer you left on your birthday and slammed
the door goodbye.

Electric Rats in a Neon Gutter

It was the night of The Blackout.

You got your wish.

Your escape route.

When you left you took the Sun and the eternal New York night light with you.

The whole city was as dark as murder.

Four nights.

We never really spoke again.

Even when you came back for your things.

I think I hear your voice on the 6 train.

I think I see your shadow walk on 2nd Avenue.

I still smell your hair and I can't sleep.

I now write blues songs in the memory of your skin.

My Puerto Rican rose of Spanish Harlem.

There's a perfect scar where your love broke its lease on the red door of the cage of my heart.

It's in the shape of a dagger.

I rub it hard with psychic fingers when I think I cannot go on, or love again.

You taught me something.

Goodbyes are inevitable, so love no matter what.

I wrote this poem in smoke signals, in holy water and gray matter.

I smeared it on the wall of the building where we used to live with a brush made from songs, letters and dead flowers.

Praying for a reader to decipher its Now.

Electric Rats in a Neon Gutter

I Was Dreaming of You

When the sunlight did pierce
the blinds and made
my eyes seek
their shelter
behind thicker lids
in the cruel morning
of the always
burning Summer
I fought to stay asleep because
I was dreaming of you.

Yes, I was dreaming of you,
you know the kind of dreams
where time doesn't make sense
and love making happens
while the walls
of your building
dissolve into water
and the clouds
turn into birds?
Your arms held me
close and I swear
I could smell you
on me.

I dreamed of your eyes.
And you said
you missed me
and it was as though

you had never left.
And we sang
as we walked
through the otherworldly
green treed tunnels
on the streets
of your neighborhood.

Yes, I was dreaming of you
when the sun came through
the blinds
and tore
my vision open
and strangled
our
perfection.

Electric Rats in a Neon Gutter

My Blurred History

It was the early evening's drunken memory
that drew your shape on my unhinged curtains
and blew twilight kisses through my sullen door.
That is when I unlocked the locks and felt your jolts
upon the PM altar that we built.
I couldn't help but see to see and feel to feel
what we had had before.
Over my rupturing heart muscles,
my overfed yet undernourished brain cells,
before my jaded vision and speculation
I purged myself of any doubts
when our breaths danced and fought each other close,
too close not to fall
in bed-spinning, sweat stained, high octane love.
Once more my promise told its secrets, broke its vow
of silence and sacrificed
all it ever knew because we have a history, a genesis.

My memory keyed the lock again and the fire in my
guts said yes to you
and I spilled it all on the dirty tiles
of the too late kitchen in the apartment
that dares not forget and does not quite remember.

The Heart's Tangled Jungle

He was a fearful hunter
in the heart's tangled jungle.
He made preparations
for failure but didn't show them.
Ever.
He ripped off time
and charged his wallet
and his watch
for the left over crumbs
of his unfinished business.
He would write promises
to God
to be good
and pure
but his scribbled notes
were unreadable
at the moments when it counted.

He walked through gardens
with his cousins
telling half truths
as their grandma's chiles ripened
and magnolias kept their mouths shut
and the roses were busy
being perfect.

In those lonely moments
when there was no one to lie to
and no reason,

Electric Rats in a Neon Gutter

he would tell himself
that everything
was going to be alright
and the wind in his blinds
and the Virgin Mary candles
tried to tell him
the truth.
All the truth
for the lonely hunter
kept the sun on his face
but no light, no light
no grace
to signify
that he
was walking,
talking
right.

The Cold in August in Houston

I will never forget the last time I saw you.
You were telling me to leave
and I could tell that you meant it
this time.
It was in the middle of the day
in the middle of August
in the middle of Houston.
The sun beat me like a dog,
like every regret
I ever had and every lie I ever told
and every promise I ever broke
all at once, like a suit made of
suffocation and pain.
It was also humid.
I remember you standing in the merciless heat
of the Summer's break up,
the too early end, the final goodbye.
You stood in the front yard
and looked at me
with such pity and disappointment.

I reeked of Vodka, cigarette smoke,
self-hatred and shame
and every lie I ever told, every broken promise,
every unkept appointment,
every pleading and prayer
came to collect
all at once.
Your goodbye was the bill.

Electric Rats in a Neon Gutter

I didn't have enough to pay it
and I left in every direction
but the one that I wanted to go in
which was back to you
with one last I'm Sorry.
My Forever's and Love You's melted
right then and there in the cold
in the middle of the day
in the middle of August,
in the middle of Houston.

Crucifix Mountain

Did you see me up on
crucifix mountain
wearing my Che Guevara t-shirt
and reciting Juan Felipe Herrera?

I was waiting there with the
Pistoleros of the Roaring Dawn
and the Cholo Raiders from
the wrong side of Everywhere...

We come together in that place
to sing hymns to Quetzalcoatl.
We make sacrifices under the new moon.
We drink the herb that dissolves all boundaries.
We see things for what they are.

As the veil is peeled away
we see the truth.
There is only one moment.
This one.
To be brown and enlightened
is the quest...

The road is long
and my synapses are old and rusty.
But I got heart.
I got a big ol' engine for a
motherfuckin' heart and
it is as true as gospel.

Electric Rats in a Neon Gutter

Cruising in my '64 Impala
through the gates of eternity.

El Tafito

Those eternal days on that sunburned street
on the brown side of town.
From First Street to La Placita.
Where the vatos locos ruled and church bells rang
loud.
Where manhood was formed in a twisted wind
on the puny playgrounds of the Catholic shadows.
Where cruelty ran the show.
Where your skin didn't matter in your hood but did
everywhere else.
Where venomous children bit and stank in the Texas
sun.
If there was a time I could rewrite
it would be the ones where I would cower
in my sad and tiny room on the heat buckled floor
hiding in absolute terror of everything.
Fear of being too brown.
Fear of not being brown enough.
Forget Spanish. Learn English.
Wishing it were not this way.
Any way but this.
Not being tough enough to laugh
and too scared to piss in the stalls
for fear of ese bullies and cholo stranglers.
Knives and fireworks,
boots and broken teeth.
Black eyes and playground challenges.
Witches in the trees in the high noon daylight.

Electric Rats in a Neon Gutter

Lechusas on starless nights perched on fences outside
the window.
Whispering your name.
Brujeria!
Challenged to fight an unwinnable brawl.
Walking through the barrio like a frightened
gunslinger.
Called out on a sunny day.
Fight or be shamed forever.
Then, at last, respite.
Homemade tortillas and beans and chile
made my ribs and heart happy for a moment...
Happier than the dope fiends and winos
on the corner of Juarez and Davis
in the holy shadows of the steeple
of Our Lady of the Immaculate Conception.
My eyes burned to see something else.
I falsified my courage.
I forged my toughness with my Father's name.
My scrawny ass would not waver on the way to la
tienda.
To buy him cigarettes.

Jesus Es El Senor
Jesus Te Bendiga
Save me once, please?
The brown side of town burned daily.
The Sun beat me down.
The sun beat us Brown.

A Moral Hustler

Say young blood, let me holla at you for a minute. You look like a young man who knows a good deal when he sees it. I got this gold chain for sale. Is it real? Hell yeah it's real! It's legit. I ain't nothin' but legit, baby. Now I am prepared to let it go for a very, very reasonable price. Now dig this, I don't know where it came from, and I don't know who stole it but rest assured it is stole. This shit is hot like cayenne pepper. That's right young blood this shit is illegal like a motherfucker.

Now as I was saying I am prepared to give it away for twenty dollars. And that's the golden price, the friend price. You my friend, young blood, you my golden homie, homie!

So what you say? You want it? It will look dope on your neck. Rope a dope, that's right, like a chick lasso, a chick magnet. Make a girl notice quick, quick like a chick flick.

So what's that? You'll take it?

Good.

Before you take it, dig this: you have a choice to make and that choice will set off a string of events and maybe these events will have dire consequences and repercussions, maybe not. They call that the butterfly effect, dig? You may rip a hole in the muthafuckin' time-space-continuum. So now you unsure, huh? I understand, that's some heavy shit. Well, while you diggin' that dig this also: I'm hungry, hungry and thirsty. I can get me a bottle of sweet syrup and a taco, and a pack of them cheap ass smokes, and it don't matter to me cause a smoke is a smoke. Hell, I'll sleep well tonight. You want me to sleep well don't you? You look like a fine young fellow with good intentions, a good heart. A golden heart, yes? So think about it, young blood, think hard, but not too hard, the sun's goin' down quick and that syrup will keep me warm.

Listen golden homie, I don't know what to tell you. You can either take it, or leave it, but if you take it, you can't leave it. Takin' it means you took it, it's yours. Leavin' it relieves you of all responsibility and there is nothing else to be said about it. Take it. Leave it. All it costs you is the weight you assign to the choice and the choice will make you who you are so be careful.

Either way twenty bucks is a good price.

Adios Chica Linda *(Song in the Key of E)*

I've got my boots,
I've got my song,
I've got my black leather jacket
cause the world is cold, the road is long.
Lighting out for the territories trying to be free
want to see all the things this country boy can see
Most of all I want to put some distance 'tween you
and me.

I've been sick
and I've sure been tired
I've been up, down, below the ground,
I've been stoned, drunk and wired
I've had every occupation that a man can hold,
I've lost every single thing but my heart and soul
and I sure got a bunch of problems, or so I'm told.

Don't you dare say that you understand me,
you'll probably up and cut out just as fast as you can,
you'll see.
Aww baby, you won't even miss me.

Next time you look me up
well you just might find
I'm just a bonafide wacko
ponderin' space and time.
I've cut my losses
bore my crosses
all the way down to Corpus Christi,

Electric Rats in a Neon Gutter

it's no mystery that you don't even miss me.
That's okay because I'm doing fine here in LA.
Baby it's true,
I'll say Adieu,
I don't love you like I used to.

The Dead Beat Hero on the Broken Edge of Town

This dead beat hero
on the broken edge of town
with holes in his overgrown shoes
lies to the day that he will be cool.
So cool in fact that
the girls will not realize
how bad he smells
how often
he shoots people
how rarely
he sees his children
or his P.O.
His wives will clamor
in the big brown barrio
all night long
like lechusas from Robstown.
His mariachi melancholy
has no expiration date.
His khakis have stains and creases.
He will make promises to his friends
on unemployment day.
The first and fifteenth for sure homes!
He will not starve to see the sun.
He will not yell to the homies
when he sees five-o
creep through the hood with their lights off.
He will hustle the moon
for the silver in its beams
in the pachuco night

Electric Rats in a Neon Gutter

underneath the cholo stars
and undertake
heroics on the paycheck penetrations
of half priced hoes
in the back of his El Camino
with no bumpers
on a flea market poncho
made in Taiwan
all the while howling
like Vicente Fernandez " Volver !Volver!"
with tequila eyes
and pinata skin
in the Mexico of his Mind.

Beggin' and Pleadin'

Come on baby,
give me your love
one more time.
Please,
I'm beggin' you baby.
Just put it on me
once more.
Like a blanket,
like a suit,
like a blessing.

Let me feel
your skin on my skin
let me run
through your scent like a child in the breeze
let me shout
in your valley
let me explore
your features
let me lose
my mind in your hair
your teeth, your ankles, your face.

It's all I want,
all I need.
I want to make
the dawn itself
knock on the door
and say, "Guys can you keep it down in there?

Electric Rats in a Neon Gutter

There's children, church-goers
and lonely people out here.
Your noises are making them nervous.
One of them has fainted!"

Put your love on me
like a champagne bubble bath.
Put your feelings into it
and make me dizzy, giddy
with your moans and groans,
your bites and slaps.
Pour me all the way
to nirvana baby,
take me with you
all the way
to the end.
Pour me to sleep
and wake me up again.
C'mon baby, just one more time.
It's the only way to live.
It's the best way to die.

Right on Cortlandt

You took me to the rooftop
and strangled me with your kisses
your eyes promised
soft purple sheets and fantasies
that to this day
cause me to moan aloud
at the memory of that time
when you pulled me close
in the Hot Houston Night
and kissed me first.
Hard.
My insides howled
like a pagan choir.
You told me, not asked me,
to go home with you.
My blood turned outlaw
on a dime and I would've
sold myself to the lowest bidder
for one more hour
one more kiss,
for one more night
to be ripped to pieces
and made whole again
by the beauty of your face
by the deep hunger of your eyes
by the smell of your room
by the sweet ache of that time
by the memory
of that night.

Electric Rats in a Neon Gutter

I followed you.
I followed
and followed
you there.
On Cortlandt street
take a right
and keep
on
going...

NYC

He awoke before the sun on a Tuesday, or was it Wednesday? No, Tuesday. His apartment was dark and cold. The window was not black with night, which was one of the last things he remembered from the previous evening, but slate gray, dull, pigeon-wing gray with the approaching morning. He would have been consumed by the cold completely had he not been lying next to her. Her body was more than warm and she breathed deeply with the alcohol and exhaustion from the night before. The last thing he remembered was making love to her and passing into a deep sleep completely naked under the sheets. He kissed her twice on the cheek and held her close as he dissolved into sleep again. He was more than happy, he was at ease, peace. His hope as he drifted into that same sleep was that their dreams would intertwine in the ether of the realm of rest. Time vanished and The Earth hung suspended in The Universe, slowly turned and spun him to sleep.

He awoke again several hours later and she was not in bed. Several minutes passed like that, in a cool blue silence. He heard footsteps approaching his room and she appeared in his black sweatshirt from the night before and nothing more.

She quickly crawled up his body and nuzzled his neck. She said good morning and kissed him. She said she wanted breakfast and that she wanted to go to the park. He said it was a good idea even though the temperature had to be in the low thirties.

They made love again then got dressed slowly and without effort. They walked out the front door of the building and into the clear blue day. It was cold and bright. New York City never looked more vibrant, more beautiful, more right.

He was severely hung over but didn't care, after all it was always this way. Every day, every week and every month for as many years as he could count on one hand. The only difference now was that he didn't have to do it alone. They were a perfect match. They matched each other drink for drink drug for drug smoke for smoke and long deep kiss for long deep kiss.

They walked to the McDonald's on 111th Street and Third Avenue. They ordered two breakfast sandwiches with hash browns and two coffees. They faced west and began walking toward Central Park. They crossed the street and headed south to 110th Street, turned right and headed west again. They passed Lexington Avenue, passed Madison to Fifth Avenue and then walked directly through Duke Ellington square underneath the bronze statue of Sir Duke and his piano to the Northeastern most corner of Central park.

At 110th Street and Fifth Avenue was a small pond by a large steep hill called Harlem Meer. There were steps and benches on the edge of the pond where ducks and swans glided along the surface of the water. They walked to the edge of the pond and situated themselves on a bench facing the water. They unpacked their breakfast and ate slowly but hungrily. The food was warm and the coffee was hot.

When they finished the food he crushed the wrapping paper of the breakfast sandwiches in his hands like he was packing a snowball. He put the ball into the bag which held the sandwiches and crumpled the whole thing again. He stood up and walked to a nearby trash can, threw the trash in and returned to the bench. When he sat she offered him a smile and a kiss. They sat there in silence, drank their coffee and watched the ducks and swans slowly paddle along in front of them.

How do you feel about us? she asked. About how our relationship is going? Was it too soon to tell you that I love you? I don't think it's possible, he said. Love happens when it happens, there's no speed limit, it's not a street. I love you too and it happened when it happened, we happened when we happened. I hope it lasts, she said and then she took a sip of coffee. Me too, he said. It usually never does, she said. People lie or leave or hurt you and it goes away. He turned to look at her in the eyes, I will never leave, lie or hurt you, I promise. She looked back at him with question on her face. The wind was blowing and it dried their eyes to the point of tears. Did you know that swans mate for life? she asked. They choose a partner and they stay with that partner no matter what until one of them dies. Then when one of them dies the other one does not take another partner. The one that is left then dies alone. Swans are better than people. They don't lie, they don't hurt each other and they are faithful. Swans are better than us because they don't fuck each other over the way that we do. They are perfect and when they swim together and when they fly, they fly with one another. There is this picture that I saw once where there are swans and they are kissing and the shapes that their necks and their heads make forms the shape of a heart. It's like God made them beautiful and true to show us how to be, how we should be, could be. We are not swans, he said. I love you and that is all I know. I think about us and how we fell in love so quickly, because that is what happened, at least that is the way it happened to me. I fell in love I mean I fell like, splash, crash, down and up, like that wino that we saw at 86th Street that fell off the subway platform? That's how I fell for you. So I fell and now you have me, you have my undivided attention and truthfully I don't want to divide my attention anymore, you are my attention. Us, we, this, you and me. And even though I ain't perfect like a swan, I know my love for you is perfect. I didn't have anything to do with it. It was like the angels put you in my life and when I saw you, I fell. Hard. You were so beautiful that day and I knew, I knew that I would love you and I did, but I ain't no swan. I know, she said. They sat there at the water's edge and watched the ducks and swans for a long time, in silence. Not an uncomfortable silence but one filled with a quiet understanding and daydreams about what their futures might hold, how those futures would be held and who was doing the holding.

Electric Rats in a Neon Gutter

At night I walk the streets
of the city and pass the
mutants as I go.
Looking for the muse.
We together in the bony,
narrow lanes
of Hollywood
Holly Weird,
Holly what?

Night slams down
hard
and these entities scatter
like electric rats in a neon gutter.
I walk faster
hurry through
the wolf ticket fog
while English, Spanish,
Armenian and Thai fly
over me where the stars
you can't see
should be.
Sweat runs down
my left temple.
A rumble in the intestines.
A voice croaks out through crooked teeth
from a lost creature
in the half light
of the steel blue night.

"Hey homie, you got a dollar?"
"No, man, I wish."
The liquor store explodes
and bleeds hatred
desperation and dreams
onto the corner
of Serrano Avenue
and Sunset Boulevard
as I make my way home
and try to write what I have seen.
I can't.
I can't put my head
around the dizzy.
My mind does the sclerosis waltz
on the dead end page
as I search for answers
in oceans of ink
and think.

Electric Rats in a Neon Gutter

Highway 181

I'm going to let that last remark of yours slide because I have something very important to ask you. I need to be clear-headed for this but if you push me I will fuck you up entirely, period end of short-ass fucking discussion; pack some nice clothes for your funeral, I don't care. If I get to that point, that "edge" you know that "edge"? The one I am so perilously close to jumping off of or being pushed over? Once upon that edge there is a choice to be made. Now YOU have a choice.

If you ever mention what happened between me and Elaine again or if you even think it, or I even sense that you are thinking it I will make that choice for you. Make no mistake the repercussions will be severe, death will seem a daydream and the rest of your waking hours will be spent in intense agony and the deepest darkest regret that the human condition will allow; you will rue the day that you did not heed my warning and make a more well informed decision.

What happened between me and Elaine is between me and Elaine and God; and our respective lawyers, and judge Jozwick of San Patricio county, and Garza's Bail Bonds and our families and our kids and Child Protective Services and the arresting officer whom I struck during his feeble-assed attempt to apprehend me, but that's Our business and Our business alone.

Now for what I have to ask you: I need you to give me fifteen hundred dollars to buy Elaine an engagement ring. I'm going to ask her to marry me. What can I tell you? We're in Love. Anyway I need the money now and while you're sitting there wondering how close I am to the aforementioned edge of doom and fury know this shit hard: I know it was you who called the cops on me.

So can you give me my fucking money now? Please.

Electric Rats in a Neon Gutter

Brown

I walked along the brown border of your town
I saw brown workers churning away
in the splintered sun
I felt the acrid vapors of Hate's fire
flash upon the mountains to the north
I saw Hate itself on patrol,
driving a Hummer on La Cienega
I rode the dawn to the ocean
and watched it crack and fall to pieces again.

Another day with a boot on the neck
I wept pure brown tears
I sang songs of my brown ancestors
I ate the brown ideas of the barrio
like tacos de asada
I swam the brown river
from Matamoros to Brownsville
I drank the brown water
as I splashed my way to "freedom"
this was Mexico
this is Mexico
as I wind my brown watch
with brown fingers
as brown hours
drip from my brown wrist
like tequila anejo,
brown sweat runs down
my brown temples.

I feel Hate's eyes on my shoulders like claws
I see Hate's castle from my brown window
I hear your government laugh like crazed hyenas
lusting for brown blood
I hear it in my brown morning
on my brown radio
as I eat my brown eggs.

Hate, I wonder if you are real?

I hear a ringing in my ears,
a distant call
I hear Zapata, Villa and Subcomandante Marcos
singing doo-wop
from Chiapas all the way to LA
then east to el Rio Grande
and up to Corpus Christi.

Back in LA a brown baby eats a green dollar bill
as his brown mother pushed
his stroller down Cahuenga.

I saw multitudes of immigrants
flood Santa Monica Boulevard
like a brown ocean.

I see!
I see!
Mexico lindo!
Mi Tierra!

Electric Rats in a Neon Gutter

I light candles in my brown room
on this brown night
as my brown brain throbs
in my brown skull.
All my history spills on this page
like charro beans,
like brown holy water
As the brown barrio wind
sends brown angels
to lull me
to my brown dreams.

My brown soul
takes flight over Hate's dominion
all the way through
The Universe
to Heaven.

Cold Indifferent Window *(Song in the Key of G)*

Leaving Houston town again on a Northbound train to
Chicago.
Running from the memories that nailed me to the
ground
As that gray wind howled and the whistle blew a low
pitched fare thee well,
I leaned my head against a cold indifferent window.

I could tell you about the way she made me feel and
how she wouldn't say goodbye
But that wouldn't be the truth because my truth is just
someone else's lie.

Could I really change the way you feel and if I did
would I really want to?
There's damage that's been done and no one walks
away from this without some broken bones, it's true.

If you could look me in my face and in my eyes,
you'd see this ain't no joke.
But there ain't a goddamned thing that you can do
when your mind's on fire and your spirit's broke.

It seemed like the right thing to do, but the wrong
way to do it.
But my bleeding guts know more than me and they
tell me that there's nothing to it.

Electric Rats in a Neon Gutter

So I'm leaving this town for good. Yeah, I'm a liar but
now it's time to go
Because there ain't no similarity between me and a
cold indifferent window.
I see right through you like I do this cold indifferent
window.

Hubris on Your Doorknob

That night I hung
my hubris on your doorknob
and decided to stick around
and strangle your heart
with my songs
and we did drink
and dance
again and again.
Whiskey nights
and seesaw sheets
we smoked ourselves silly
and loved ourselves blind
our smells did mingle
with our lies
our stories shone
like diamonds
in the broken night under a rough
and moonless sky
your eyes still haunt me
my gray eyed Athena
my lover of plenty of time.
My whispers did rip your reason to shreds
my lies lay under your bed.
In your sink, on your rugs
in your ash trays and on your thighs.
Where did we sleep?
Did we dream away another solstice
and wild ourselves
to the next level of being?

Electric Rats in a Neon Gutter

Dreaming Awake

More and more the day stitched me into an upright
position
and your bells rang and let me live once more.
I stood in the naked perfume of your bedroom
and I drank unleaded wine at your dinner party.
I resolved to surrender to your blissful chatter.
I wondered if the moon from last night was still there.
I wondered if we were here.
I opened my eyes again and you were gone.

Like I Did Before *(Song in the Key of C)*

I spend all of my time wounding everything that heals
with too much vodka and pain pills
I believe I'll stop running out here in the west
but I don't believe I did my best.

I believe I'd like to start things over
I believe my spirit is scarred right down to the floor
I believed everything that you told me
but I don't believe you now like I did
before.
I catch my shirt on the knob as I walk out the door.

I can see South Texas in my mind
through pot residue
and empty bottles of wine
I believe I left things turned
upside down
now this king of fools will have to
wear his crown.

You don't need to explain things to me
I deserve it and I don't but that's the way it goes.
Late at night I can't sleep as this city growls away
near your bed Buffalo Bayou weeps into Galveston
Bay.

Electric Rats in a Neon Gutter

A Pipeliner's Dilemma

YOU CAN DO THIS FOREVER.

He stopped the truck and threw it into park on a dirt road just after The Universe punched him in the face. It was as though someone who was sitting next to him had reared back and struck him across the jaw line, so clear and startling was the revelation.

He'd been working on the pipeline for several months now - an outfit called King Pipeline. His younger brother had got him the job, even managed to secure him a place on his crew in those first months. They worked together in the chemical plants and refineries of Pasadena and Channelview. It was good to work with his brother. He enjoyed it very much. But his brother had recently been sent to head up a new job in New Orleans, leaving him alone to work with men he did not know on a cattle ranch on the outskirts of nowhere while living in a cheap motel room in Goliad, Texas.

He'd started on the pipeline in the early Summer of that same year, a month after graduating from a university on the East Coast with an Master of Fine Arts in Fakery and Disguise. He'd vowed that he'd never take another job where he'd have to shower after work - just a few years before, sitting in his apartment in New York City with his friends, proposing a toast, "Here's to grad school boys and to never having to lift shit for a living again." But since then he'd done much lifting, continued lifting and had been lifting heavy objects until just a few moments before The Cosmos had tried to give him a knockout blow in the cab of the work truck which he now drove.

He'd just completed a ten-hour workday on the Polinski Cattle Ranch where he and the pipe gang were laying half a mile of thirty-two inch pipe, which was to be pulled underneath the San Antonio River then used to transport natural gas to its final destination. Where that destination was he didn't know or care.

As he sat in the cab of the work truck alone, a mile away from the main gate of the ranch he began seeing things in a different light and thinking things with a different means of process. The truck, the sky. The whole world seemed very familiar yet strangely different, more wondrous than it ever had, before this moment. And in a voice as clear as his own he heard the voice again, *You could be happy doing this for the rest of your life. Maybe.*

The sun was setting and it streaked the South Texas sky with swaths of purple, pink, orange and blue the likes of which he'd never seen before in his life. Cattle grazed lazily on that vast stretch of land. Pecan and Mesquite trees dotted the ranch as far as one could see to the south. Small flocks of birds winged through the twilight. Though the truck's engine was off the radio still played low, but clear. It was a country music station and the song was pure honky-tonk heartbreak. Steel guitars cried and a man's voice pleaded. The song, as far as he could tell, was about loss and moving on. Hands on the wheel. The enormous silence underneath absolutely everything - the light, his breath, the tightness of the muscles in his back and his legs all the way down to his steel-toe boots. All of the world, there, in that perfect moment. Precise. He was there.

Maybe I could do this forever? Maybe this is all I need? Maybe working hard, making money and living in motels until the right woman came along would be alright? I could pay off my student loan, buy a new truck, buy a house and be an eligible bachelor with something to offer. Hell, I might even quit drinking and doing drugs. Then he thought through the whole list again.

Could he give up trying to be an artist? Could he really work this way for the next thirty years? Would this be enough to sustain his spirit, his comfort level, while his loftier ambitions were put on hold? Could he pretend those ambitions were not there? Could he continue pouring vodka and pills on his problems? Would the fire that burned inside him be extinguished long enough for him to build an escape route to this kind of life?

He thought of the long days of work. The sun or the cold beating him down one millimeter at a time. He would be beaten a little smaller every day. He thought of the intolerance of some, not all, of the workers on the crew, the bosses, the bosses' bosses until it became one long chain of ignorance and fear. A chain of hate forged in the cold fires of the inability to reach out, to try and understand another human being. How many more "fuckin' wetbacks" could he hear before exacting revenge?

He thought of the woman he might meet. Would he meet one that really loved him? One that read Thomas, Cummings and Shakespeare? One that would tolerate his penchant for carousing until the small hours? One that would stay?

Thought after thought, possibility after possibility. Scenarios from what he thought a normal happy life might look like flooded his head. Scenes with women, first dates, bank managers, car dealers, dentists, in-laws, doctors, children, little league games, all of these things filled his mind at once like some dry and desolate water tank with a rusty and reluctant valve which now broke open and flooded the parched and dry receptacle of his mind with hope and wonder. He looked at his reflection in the side-view mirror. He saw the face of a man he thought he knew staring back at him. A man only slightly familiar, like some distant cousin met only once or twice in childhood.

Electric Rats in a Neon Gutter

The sun had almost disappeared and the brilliant colors from a few moments ago were almost gone like ribbons being taken down after a birthday party. Deep indigo and lighter blues remained, hanging there in space like towels on a clothesline. He turned the key in the ignition. The engine started right away, a low loping murmur. He put his right foot on the brake, shifted into drive, released the brake and slowly made his way down the dirt road towards the ranch gate and its lock.

He arrived at the gate, put the truck in park and killed it. He got out, unlocked the gate and swung it open away from the highway which was just a few yards in front of him. He got back in the truck, started it, drove to through to the edge of the highway, got out and went back to shut the gate.

Before he returned to the truck he stopped and looked left on the highway then looked right. There was no traffic, no wind, nothing save the lights of the radio towers that dotted the horizon and what few stars had begun to shine. Time was swollen, pregnant with what The Universe had just revealed to him. Was it The Universe, or him? His own fear, intolerance and inability to reach out and understand another human being, namely himself?

He stood there in that dense stillness. Maybe this life isn't so bad after all? Maybe I don't need to be an artist? It could be this simple all the time. The distrust of these ideas made his shoulders tense. He drew a deep breath and sighed it out.

He needed a drink. He walked back to the truck, reached under the seat and pulled out a plastic pint bottle of vodka wrapped in an oil cloth and stored in a plastic bag. He unwrapped it and looked to see how much was left. A little less than half. Just enough to get him to the liquor store and refuel and to make the music on the radio sound better. It would also serve to help him forget the decision that was put to him, if just for the rest of the night.

He unscrewed the top and took a long hard pull. The jet-fuel vapors in the nose and the sweet burn down the throat were all too familiar to him now. He'd been drinking and drugging hard for a year now. It felt exactly right and completely wrong at the same time, like playing himself at chess and pretending not to know what his next move would be. He screwed the cap back on and shoved the bottle, rag and bag under the seat again. He got in the truck, put it in drive and headed west on the highway towards Goliad in the quiet night. The vodka had loosened his nerves like a hot bath and he turned up the radio.

The Universe had punched him in the face. The only questions left were would he punch back and how hard? He pressed the gas a little harder and watched the needle on the speedometer rise. Night was now completely upon him and he wondered what he would do.

Da.Da...Da da

Would he say yes to her
under an ancient sky
upon an ancient quest?
I want her all the time. Now. Now.
I keep these words in a red pill bottle in my brain
in that eclipsed night.
Your promise outweighed your sense.
My money flew away like birds on fire
and I did not care.
Under the absent moon with unclean eyes.
Turning back is not an option.
I want to swim in the sacred pools of her eyes.
The want raged through my spine like a train
over the big iron rainbow in my mind.
The kiss sent electric shivers to all our private places.
How can I get to the other side of this ocean?
My dilemma is as rank as diesel.
Her music filled my body.
It appears this ache is real, as real as rubies.
I want to eat her breath.
I don't know if I will ever be what I am supposed to
be.
The night thrashed in its cage like a beast
from the dark parts of space.
Unhinged from day one.
I cannot see beyond what is in front of me.
My heart pounded in my chest like a flat tire. Thump.
Thud.
On the only night we can afford.

Electric Rats in a Neon Gutter

El Chingaso Grande

The world stopped spinning
suddenly
and without
warning
as though it were
trying to avoid
some galactic collision
and at once
all the energy,
molecules, quarks
and atoms
slammed the brakes
and jolted
the fabric of creation
like a drunk driver
ramming a tree.
Time ceased to be.
Finally.
All of our matter
and meaning
was sent hurtling
forward and splattered
the inside of the windshield
of the world
after the stop
(we weren't wearing our seat belts
and this model is too old for airbags).
Religion, war,
philosophy,

political theory,
dogma,
quantum physics,
theoretical math,
the golden mean,
Love, sex,
joy, peace,
murder,
betrayal, death,
Everything splattered
and steaming
sliding down the inside
of this vehicle
like beef enchiladas,
down the cosmic dashboard
and into
the vents
of the
billion year old jalopy.
And there it lay,
stultified and prostrate
in the fabric
of the all
like a drip
of barbecue sauce
on God's
shirt sleeve
as angels
and aliens
gather like flies
to sift

Electric Rats in a Neon Gutter

the viscera.

The Puddle of Romeo's Tears

Why didn't you
Return my howls
Last night
Under the moon's
Silver chains
And pink undergarments?
Were you busy?
Were you washing
Your hair
In the tears
Of half assed Romeos
In the unrequited evening?

I was there
Under your balcony
I was wearing
A green snake skin suit
That I bought
From the
Our Mother of Holy Agony
Thrift Store
On the corner of
Mistake and Trust.
While standing there
And howling,
I could see
The sign of
The manufacturer
Of the fire escape

Electric Rats in a Neon Gutter

Under your window.
It was stamped
Into the cold
Dark steel.
It read:
Dirtyfuckinglie, Inc.

I stood there
For hours with
A love poem
I had written
The night before
On a napkin
From our favorite
Chinese restaurant.

I had planned
On reciting it
To you,
At midnight
But it was too late.
You were
Not There
You were

Elsewhere.

I crumpled it
And threw it
Into a puddle
On the street

That other Romeos
Had no doubt
Left behind.
A tiny ocean
Of broken hearted
Crybaby evidence.

I looked into
The puddle
With the light
From a match.

I saw tadpoles
With golden halos
Swimming erratically
And bumping into
One another like
A miniature
Crash up derby.

The match burned
My finger and
I let it drop.

The night had
Stolen my identity
And used it
To buy black
Market weapons
In the murky
Shadows up

Electric Rats in a Neon Gutter

Your
Private
Alley.

Las Hermanas Rios

I was raised by women
strong brown women
who sheltered me behind the barrio
barricade of their hearts.

If I told you that these women knew no fear
that would be a lie.
Their pushing through fear
to put food on the table
and clothes on my back is what
makes them brave.

I was raised by women
superhuman brown women
that put tortillas in my belly
and salsa in my veins.

They dealt with absent fathers
they dealt with no child support
they dealt with foodstamp shame
they dealt with WIC checks
and home wrecks.

I was raised by women
proud brown women
that despite the mal de ojo
they put on our fathers
our family photos would still
never resemble a Norman Rockwell painting.

Electric Rats in a Neon Gutter

They wore their skin thick
they kept my clothes clean
they held me up as high as they could
in their strong arms
while the world tried its damnedest
to break their legs
their spirit
their resolve.

While the world whipped and beat them
for their efforts
for their skin tone
for their poverty
for their platinum hearts
for their aguacate
for their arroz con pollo
for their canciones tristes
for la Virgen de Guadalupe.

I was raised by women
mystical brown women
that prayed rosaries in the night
and rubbed the evil away with eggs,
holy vows, and saintly tears.
Without bitterness.
With love unconditional.

Somewhere deep in their DNA
was Aztlan, Maya, Azteca.
Soil, corn, blood, roots of
the Sun People

Mexicana-Americanas
there beside me weeping
and praying
wearing cheap chanclas
on firm feet
on true legs
on strong thin shoulders
that held me up until
I could walk on my own.

I was raised by women
incredible superhuman women.
I owe them everything.
They are the only reason I'm here.

These strong superhuman proud mystical
brown women taught me right from wrong.
Efficiency, strength, endurance.
Honesty in the face of shame and ridicule.
They taught me to be a man.
Had I possessed a fraction of their character
I might have become one much sooner.
I am a man because they are women.

The Ghost of the Chicago Kid

I was living in Chicago
the year was 2009
it was cold as hell.
I was drunk all the time.
I was also high all the time.
I was fat, miserable and broken hearted.
I had rented an apartment
in the neighborhood of
Roscoe Village from a
middle aged man
who was kind and funny.
He had a son who was
in college who used to help
him around the property.
Fixing things, cleaning and such
he was a good kid
young, strong and hopeful.

I spent my birthday, Christmas
and New Year's Eve alone in that
place with the hellish cold
of Chicago and the wound in the
chest.

I was drunk and high again
when I heard the news.
The landlord's son had
died on New Year's Day.
I never knew what happened

to him, just that he was dead.

The landlord was destroyed.
He wept every time I saw him.
He seemed to be empty
and bereft of all light.
This was true heartbreak.
The man seemed dead.

While lying in bed one night
I heard the sound
of someone walking through the
apartment.
I had been alone for over a week
in that place and it was 3 am.

It's the kid, I thought
it's his ghost.
I sat up and said out loud,
hey kid is that you?
The steps stopped.
Kid it's me, it's me
it's ok kid, I'm sorry
about what happened
I really am.
Do what you need to do
I won't be afraid of you.
This is your dad's place
so I guess that makes it your place.
I'm sorry.
I don't know what else to say.

Electric Rats in a Neon Gutter

The steps began again
down the hall past my door
and into the basement.
Once they stopped I thought
did that really happen?
Was I dreaming?
Granted I am drunk and high
and heartbroken
but that sure as shit did
seem real.

I got up and lit a cigarette,
took a pull from the bottle
I had by my bed and listened,
nothing.
All that I could hear
was the unforgiving Chicago
wind and cold like a
razor coming through the cracks
in the window pane.

Every time I saw the landlord after
that I wanted to tell him but I
never did.
It's dangerous to
shake a man's hope and faith
like that.
That's why I remained
drunk, high and broken hearted.
That was all that I knew how to do.
I moved out a few months later.

There was no other place to go for
solace.
It was cold.
It was Chicago.

Electric Rats in a Neon Gutter

No. 50

He woke up from a nightmare on Thanksgiving night in his apartment in East Hollywood. Fear ran through him like a runaway child through the streets of some dark and dangerous city. He was sweating. His heart pounded. He couldn't remember what the dream was about. He only remembered faces, horrifying faces and voices that whispered, croaked and shrieked sounds so profoundly evil that to imagine their origins would be to see the other side of the rusted primal gate that separates sanity from oblivion and madness.

Why had he seen such horrible visions? Just a few hours earlier he was in a room full of friends enjoying Thanksgiving dinner and watching football. Now he was standing in the middle of his dark bedroom trembling. He could feel the presence of Evil all around him, it was crawling from the corners toward him, on the floor, across the ceiling and through the air closer and closer until he could almost touch it. He could smell it, it smelled of mold, struck matches, rotten vegetables. Death. He could still hear the voices whispering in his ear as though the whisperer were standing right next to him, close enough to kiss him. The voices whispered, "Now, now...."

He ran to the light switch, turned it on and looked around. Nothing. He was alone, but he could still sense someone, something was there with him, surrounding him, closer and closer from every direction. A dense cold enveloped him.

He'd decided to go for a run to shake the fear from his body and mind, decipher whether or not the menacing force that he sensed was real or a product of exhaustion or tryptophan. He quickly put on his sweat pants, his long sleeved shirt, his running shoes and skull cap. He exited his bedroom, left the light on, walked through his living room, turned on the lamp there and walked to and out the front door. He turned around, locked the front door, put the keys in his pocket and walked to the gate that led to Serrano Avenue. The air was chilly and it was already dark. He heard the usual sounds of the city - sirens, voices, traffic - but they seemed distant, insignificant.

He knew Evil was real…

He'd seen it up close and personal during a severe case of delirium tremens, a few years before. The terrible hallucinations he'd suffered then were filled with demons with voices exactly like the ones he'd just heard in his nightmare. Before the shakes got too bad he hit his knees and prayed aloud to God for deliverance. "God please help me!"

But only those evil voices replied, whispering "Too late, Too late," accompanied by screams charged with so much malevolence they finally snapped the thin thread that held what was left of his sanity in its rightful place. It was too much for him.

Too much alcohol, self hatred and fear had led him to that moment. He saw the ghosts of children, specters he could not describe if he tried and finally, the angel of death itself. It glared at him with eyes like molten rubies. The hideous chorus of voices and laughter taunted him, **drove him** over the edge and into the intensive care unit of a hospital in Houston, where he awoke, strapped down to a bed with leather bindings.

So he had no doubts about the authenticity of Evil...

He ran north on Serrano Ave, reached Hollywood Blvd, turned left and made his way west. He decided that he would run up Western to Franklin, turn right and run to Hillhurst and back again and in that time he might feel better and want to go home.

As he approached the corner of Western and Hollywood, he saw two men sitting at a bus stop. One young, one old. The older man was in an obvious state of advanced intoxication - mumbling incoherently and swaying back and forth. He was shabbily dressed in dark work pants and a black jacket that was torn at the right shoulder. The younger man was dressed in baggy khaki pants, large white t-shirt and a black bandana around his head. As the older man mumbled the younger man assured him gently, woo-ingly, "Don't worry, papi, I'm here for you. Anything you need just let me know and I'll take care of you." The older man continued swaying and mumbling like some doped up somnambulant newly released from an institution.

He passed the two men. Moments later, as he waited for the traffic light, he felt someone tap him on his right shoulder and say, "Hey."

He gasped and turned around. It was the younger man from the bus stop. The young man's eyes were dark and bottomless. He had a tattoo on the left side of his face but it was indiscernible, as though the artist might have made a mistake.

"Hey" said the young man again, "Don't worry I ain't gonna fuck with you." Then he smiled.

They stood there for what seemed like a very long time. Then the young man turned and walked away, toward the subway station entrance and boarded the descending escalator. As he sank into the belly of the city he turned back and stared at him again. They stayed locked on one another until the young man descended out of sight.

He realized he'd stopped breathing and took a long deep inhale. He bent at the waist and felt the cold grab hold of him like some dread agent arresting him for being born.

Electric Rats in a Neon Gutter

He stood upright and looked around, looked back toward the escalator where the young man had been. All that remained was the space he'd occupied which seemed to be buzzing and crackling like the magnetic field of Earth itself made tangible. An echo of malevolence.

He ran across Hollywood Blvd through a red light and against oncoming traffic. Cars slammed their brakes and honked at him as he zigzagged his way across. He kept running, north to Franklin and then right. His heart was pounding as though he'd been running at top speed for miles.

He began to pray aloud. Tears were gushing from his eyes and the lump in his throat made it difficult to say any words. What came out of his mouth was sound without meaning to anyone but himself and God.

As he prayed, he heard the voices from his dream following him like phantoms, taunting, whispering and laughing. He continued praying. He saw shadows run behind bushes that lay in front of him, saw demonic faces in the windows of cars that passed him. They leered and pointed as they went by. His sweat was cold and fear gripped him so tightly that he thought he would scream.

Then he did.

"GET THE FUCK AWAY FROM ME!!! YOU CAN'T TOUCH ME NOW, I WALK IN THE LIGHT, MOTHERFUCKERS, I RUN IN THE LIGHT!!!"

He ran. Faster and faster, past Normandie, past Edgemont. The specters slowly faded away like a fog dispersed by the first rays of a new and powerful sun. The fear diminished, a sense of peace and strength began to form at his very center. He looked around him for evidence of the dark forces but there were none.

The road ahead of him was almost empty except for a car that turned left on Vermont and then sped away. He stopped at the traffic light at Vermont. A woman and a small child were there beside him. The woman looked at him and smiled. "Happy Thanksgiving," she said.

"Thank you, you too." He replied.

The child, a little girl, looked up at him, smiled and looked away.

The light turned green and they crossed the street. He began running again. He turned right on Hillhurst and headed south.

He was about halfway home.

Electric Rats in a Neon Gutter

DT

Upon the waking from a fevered dream
I heard the roaring words that shook my night
And told my sleeping, waning mind
To set to pages their far off tales.

I crawled along the dusty halls of space
On darkened floors and sweat soaked moans
To tree the tell-tale monster's eyes
And grapple his lies with a lover's kiss.

I stood in dank and steaming thought
And prayed my fortune to its heels
That place and space and time behold
The marrow's marriage of word and blood.

If this were greater than the vacant head
The holy heart that hangs by thread,
The whispering angels of green-eyed fire
That wheel along the sky to waking,

There would I reside with words of old
Wizened men and their mustered fates
Unto a shredded nerve's connect
My soul to theirs to mark my place.

Then who would hear the muted storm
The blind fire's rage that smeared the veil
From graveyards black to prison's silver gate
In the mind's blue room on a vapor leash?

Would I speak of horrors or of light
Or might or maybe or should or would?
The cannots yes the would nots try
Or eulogize the death of a will misplaced?

When that venom is released and the stars reverse
Their longing to give meaning to a fevered dream
Would I still sing and recreate
The oldest stories with my mangled sense?

I would still dare in the stories climb
The ancient falling from heaven's womb
The splattering of everything on the sleeping eye
Waking, singing words not held in promise.

There would be time to ransack destiny
And fall from high to the end
And always is a place uncharted
By those who would lie themselves awake.

Electric Rats in a Neon Gutter